Barbier's Art Deco Erotica

exotic adult coloring

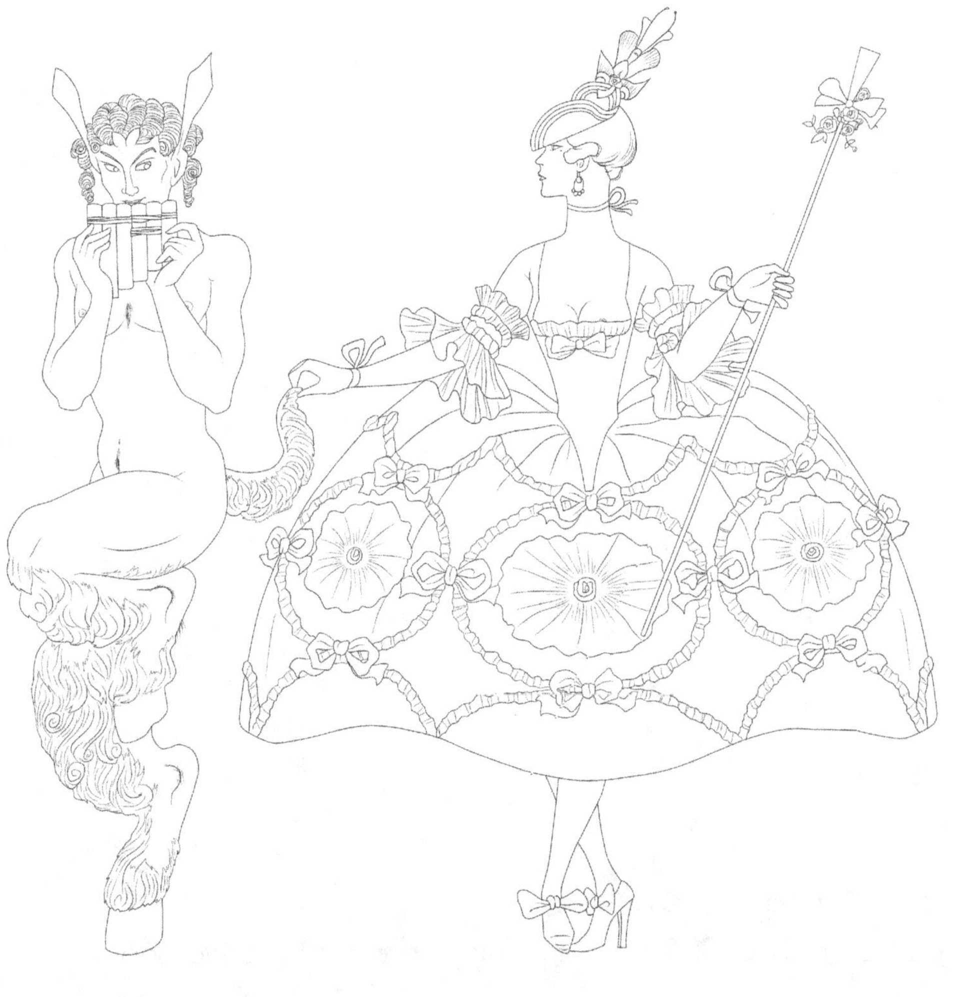

by natalie tate

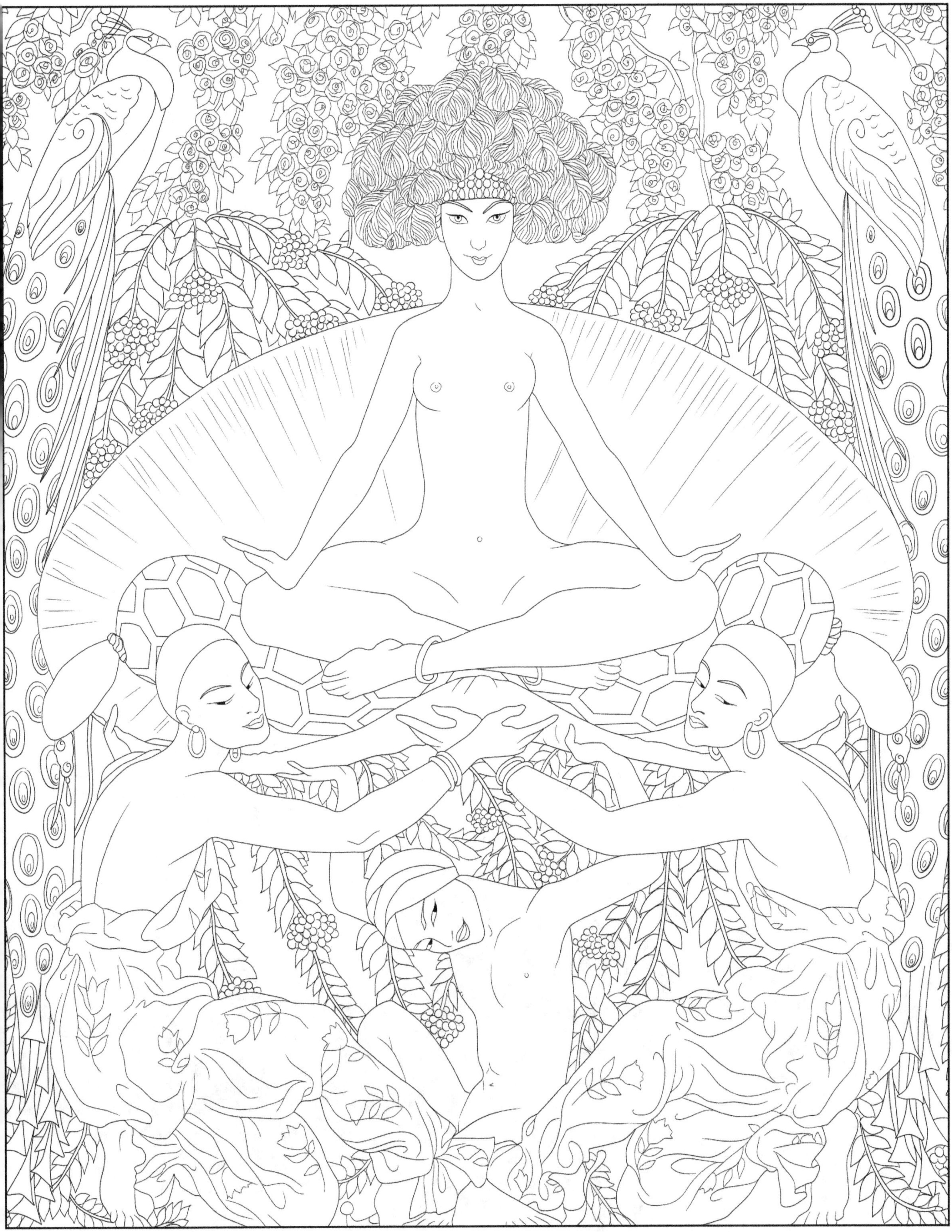

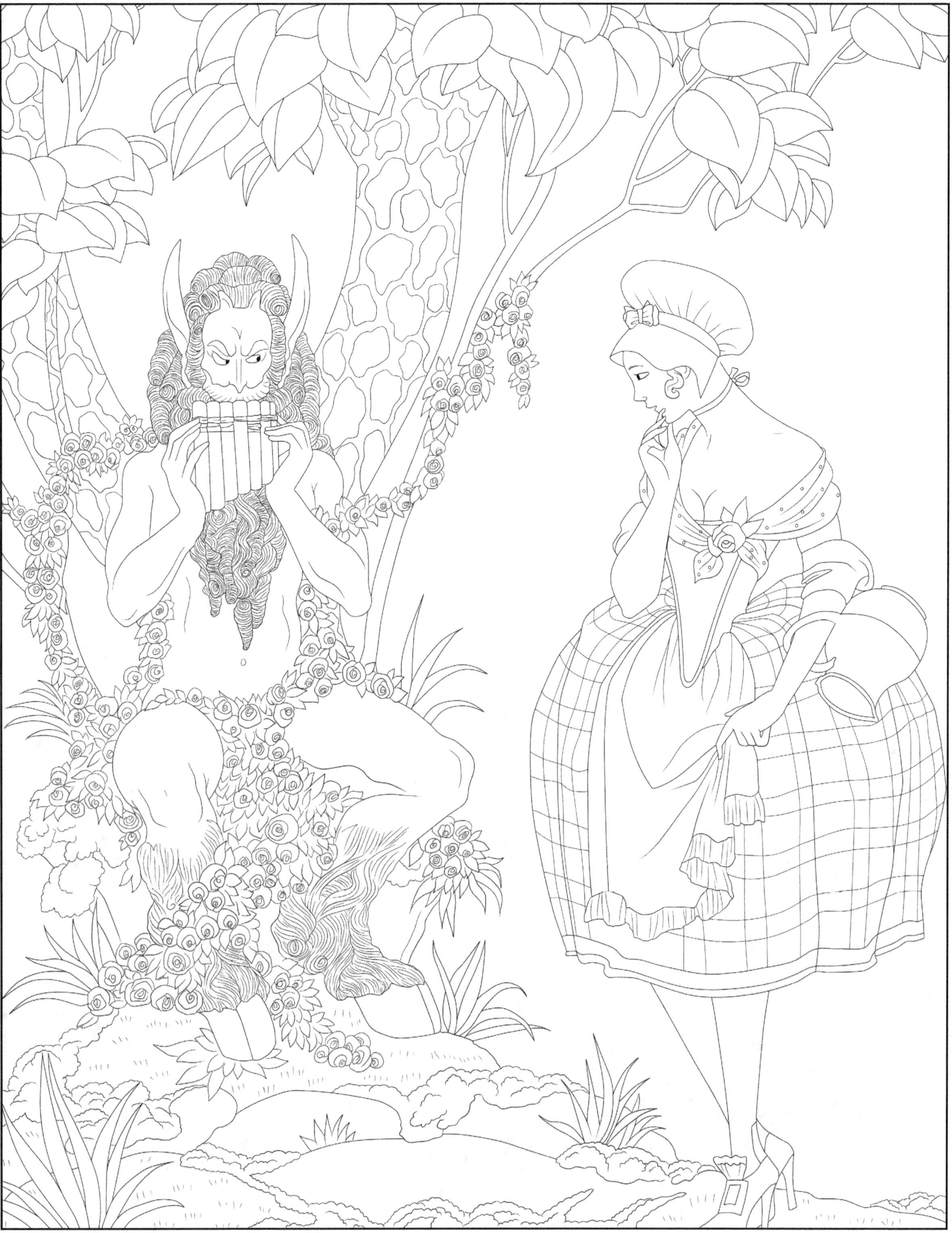

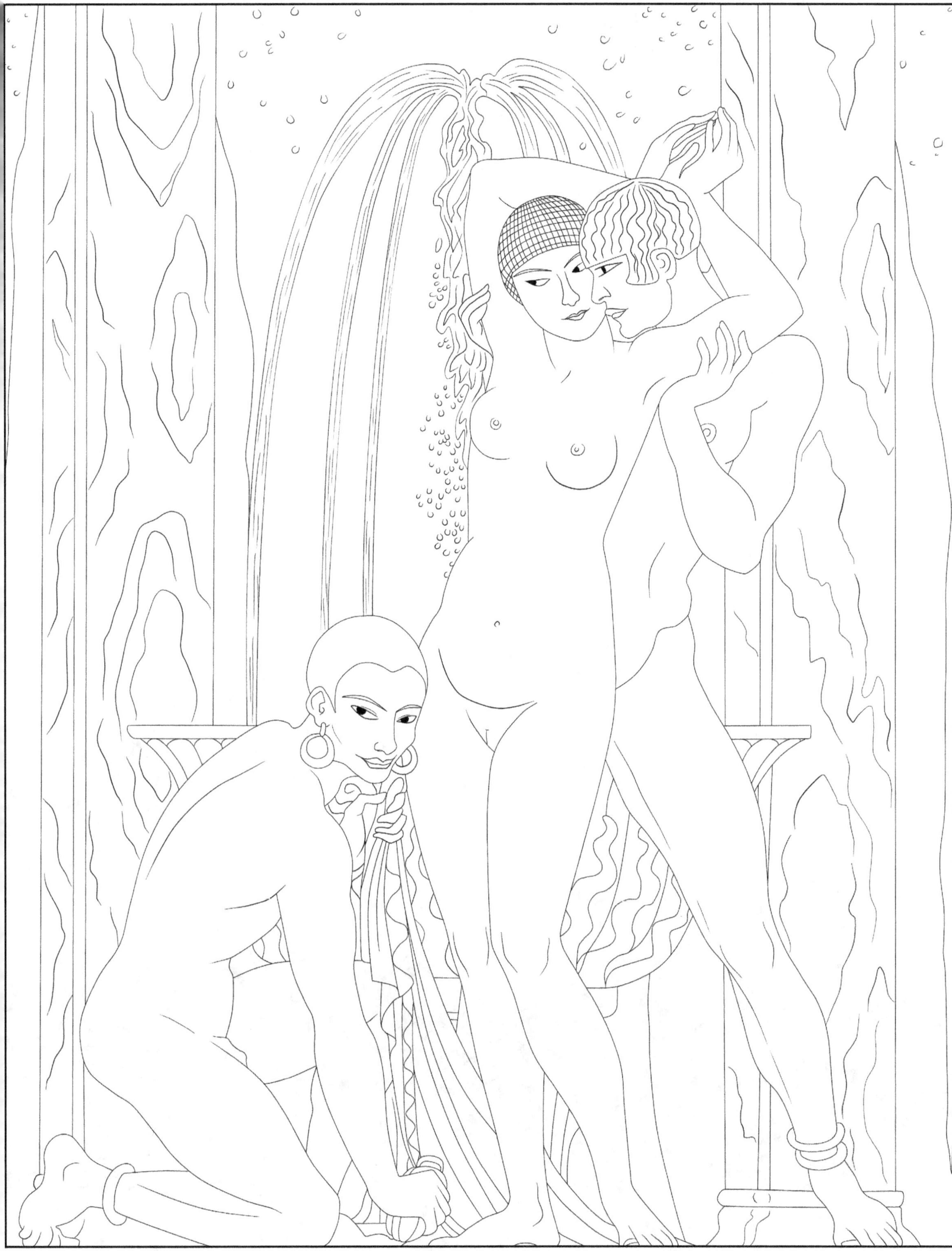

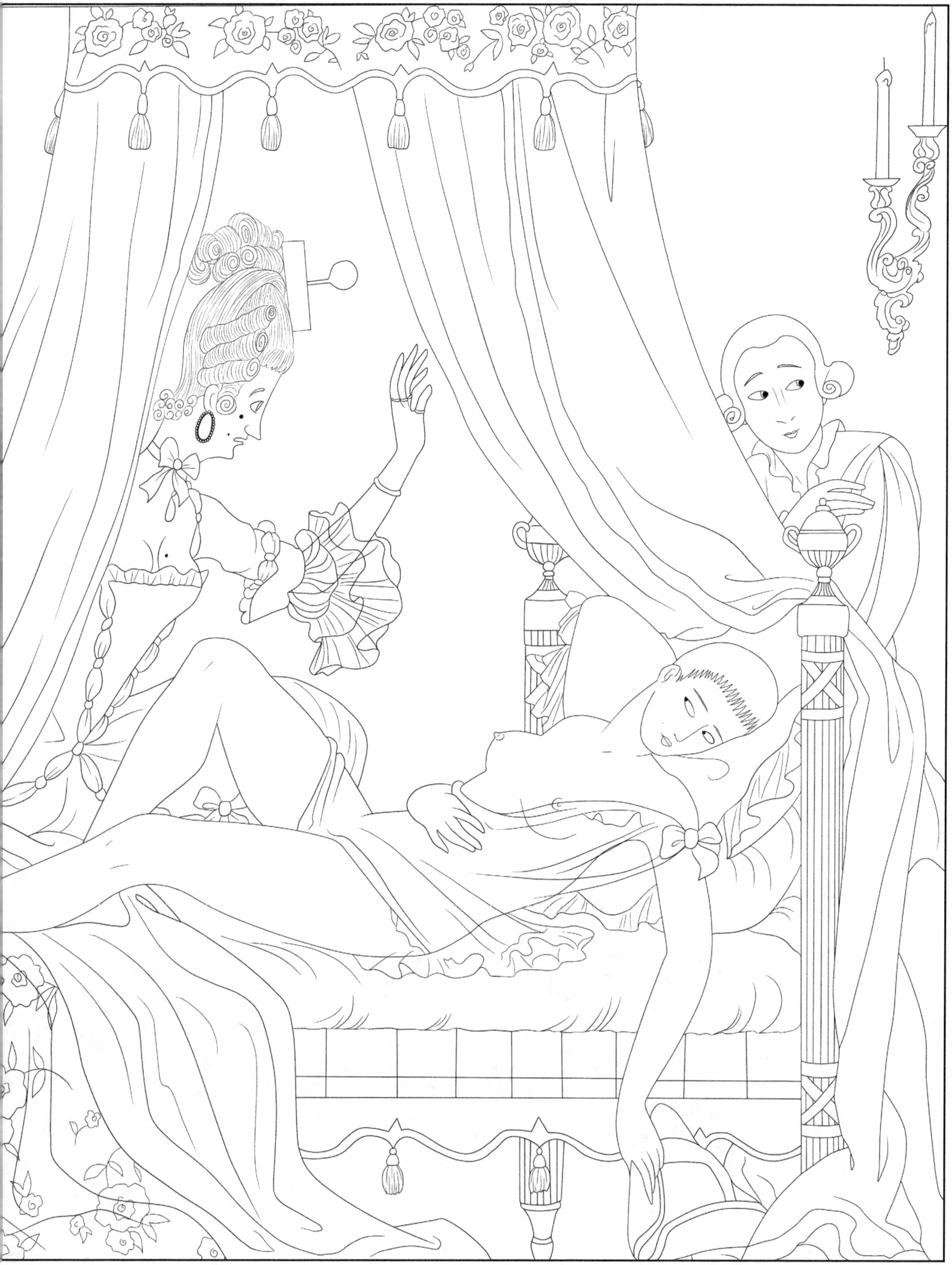

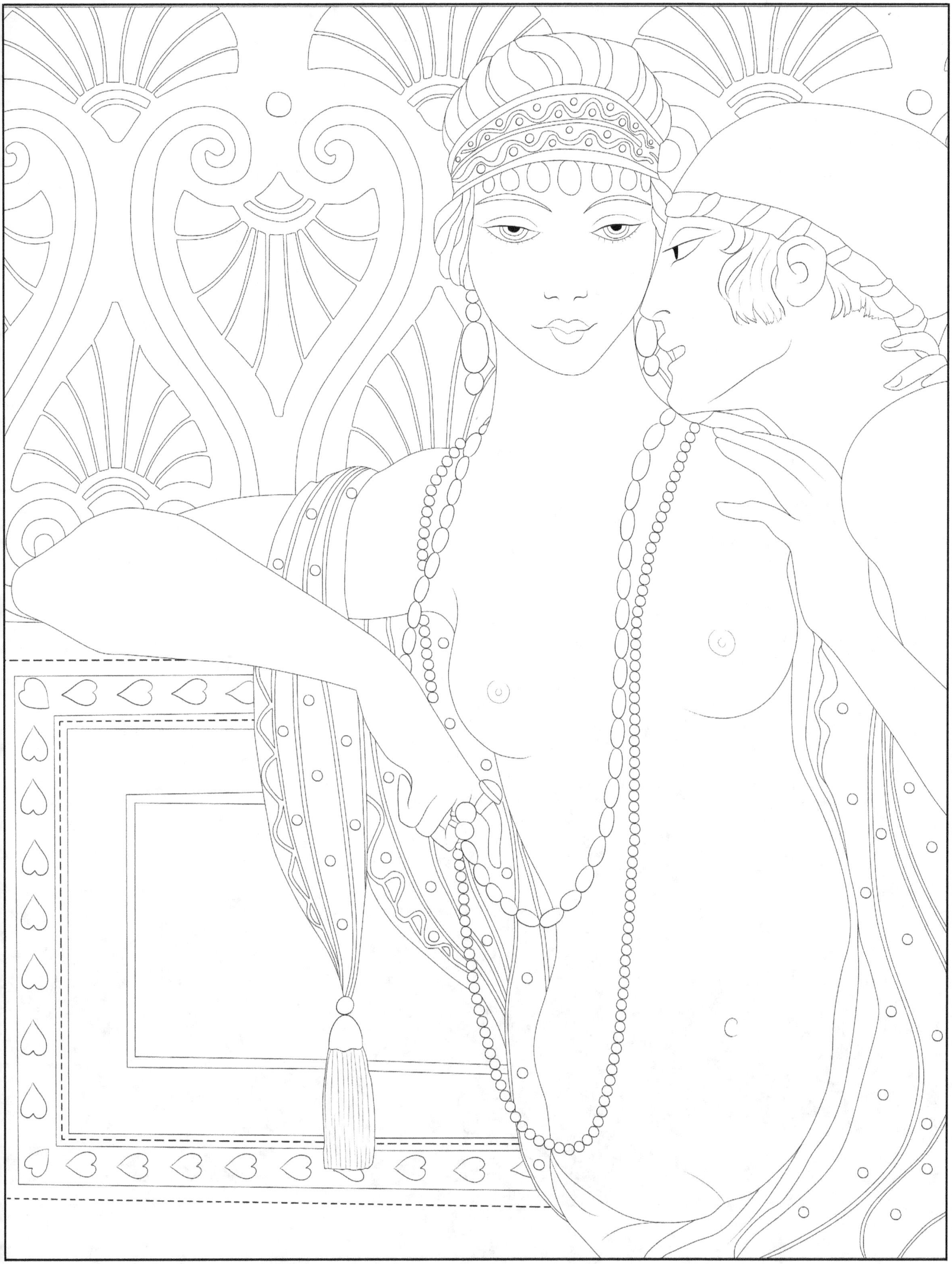

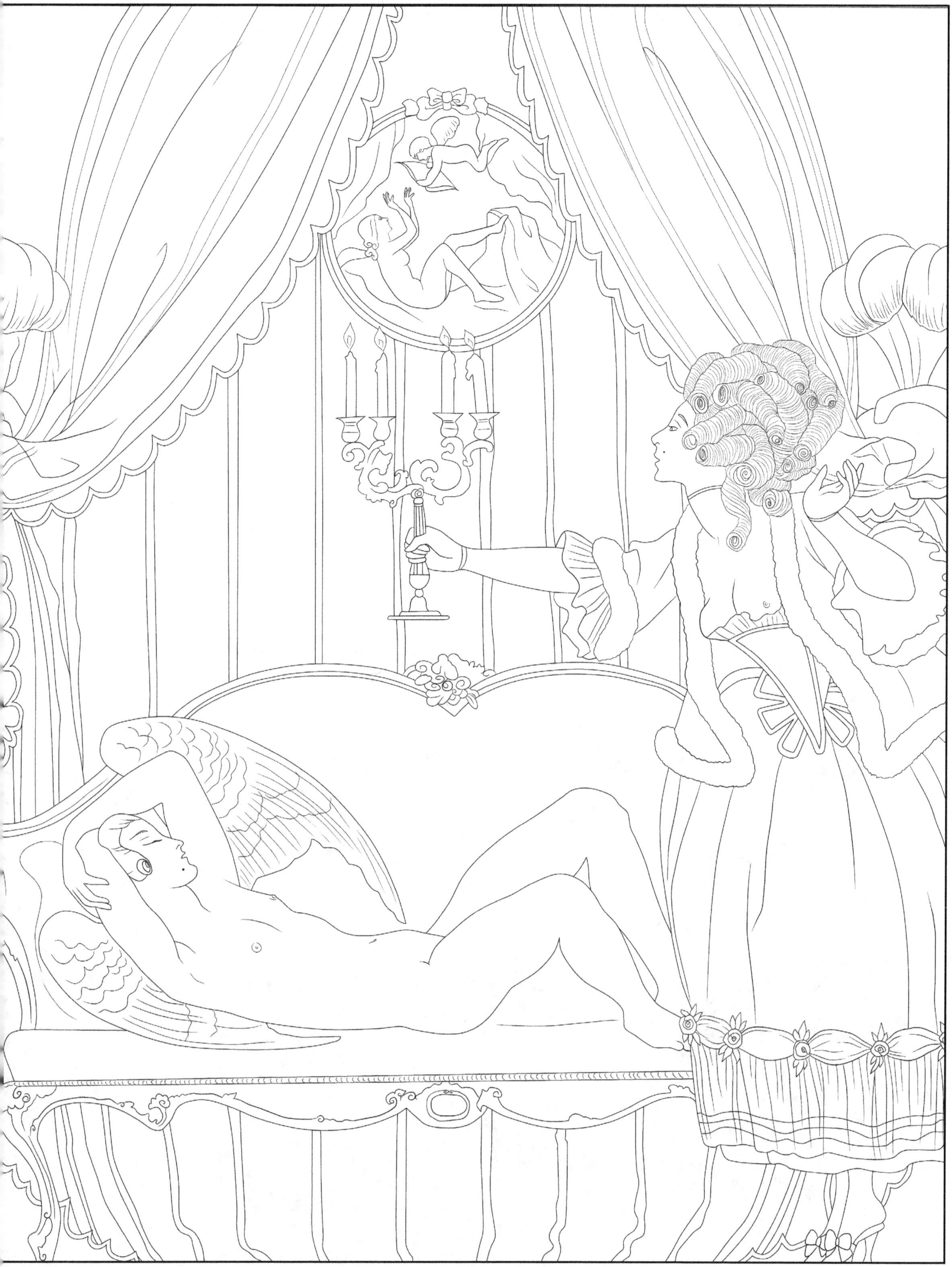

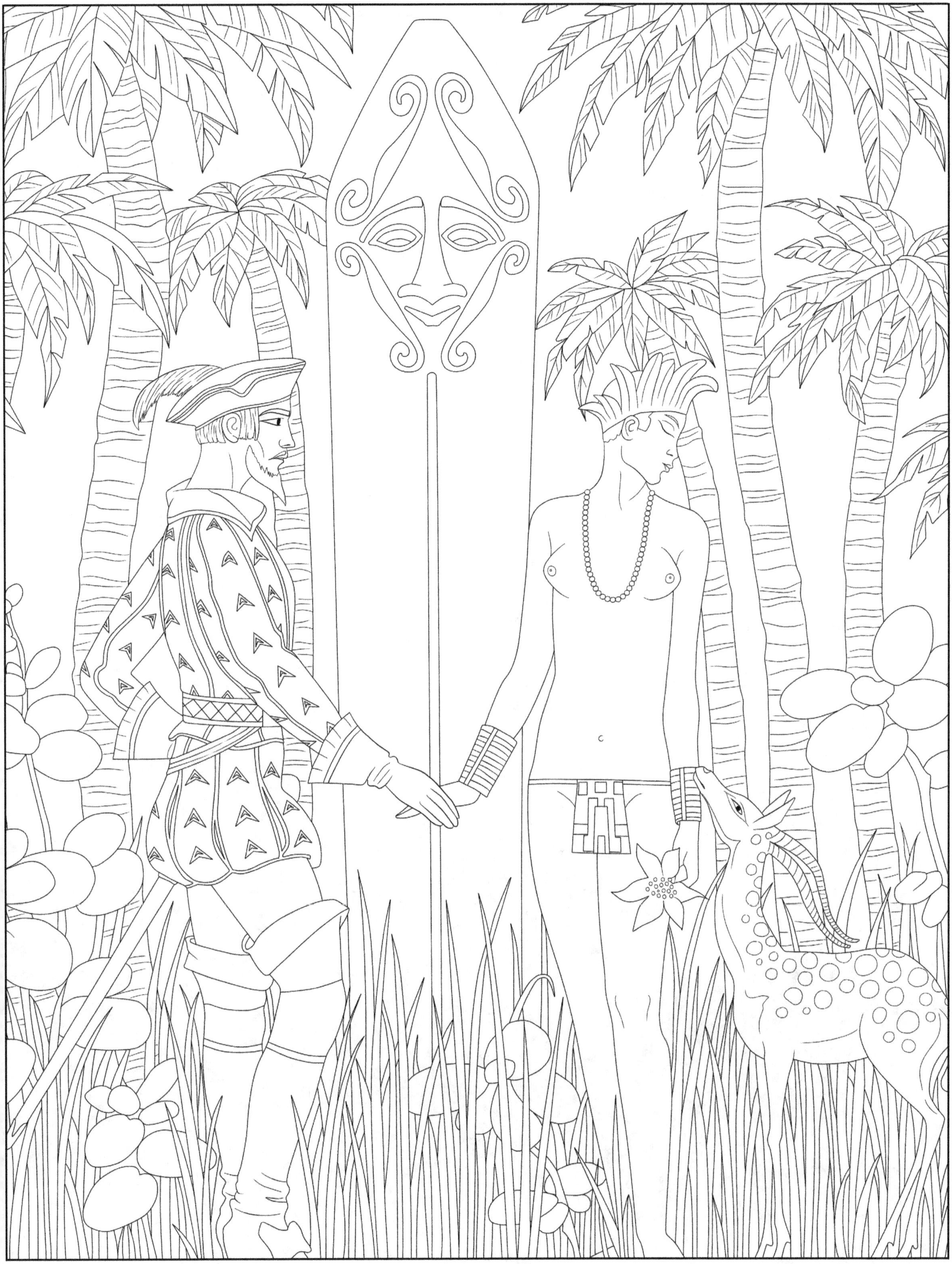

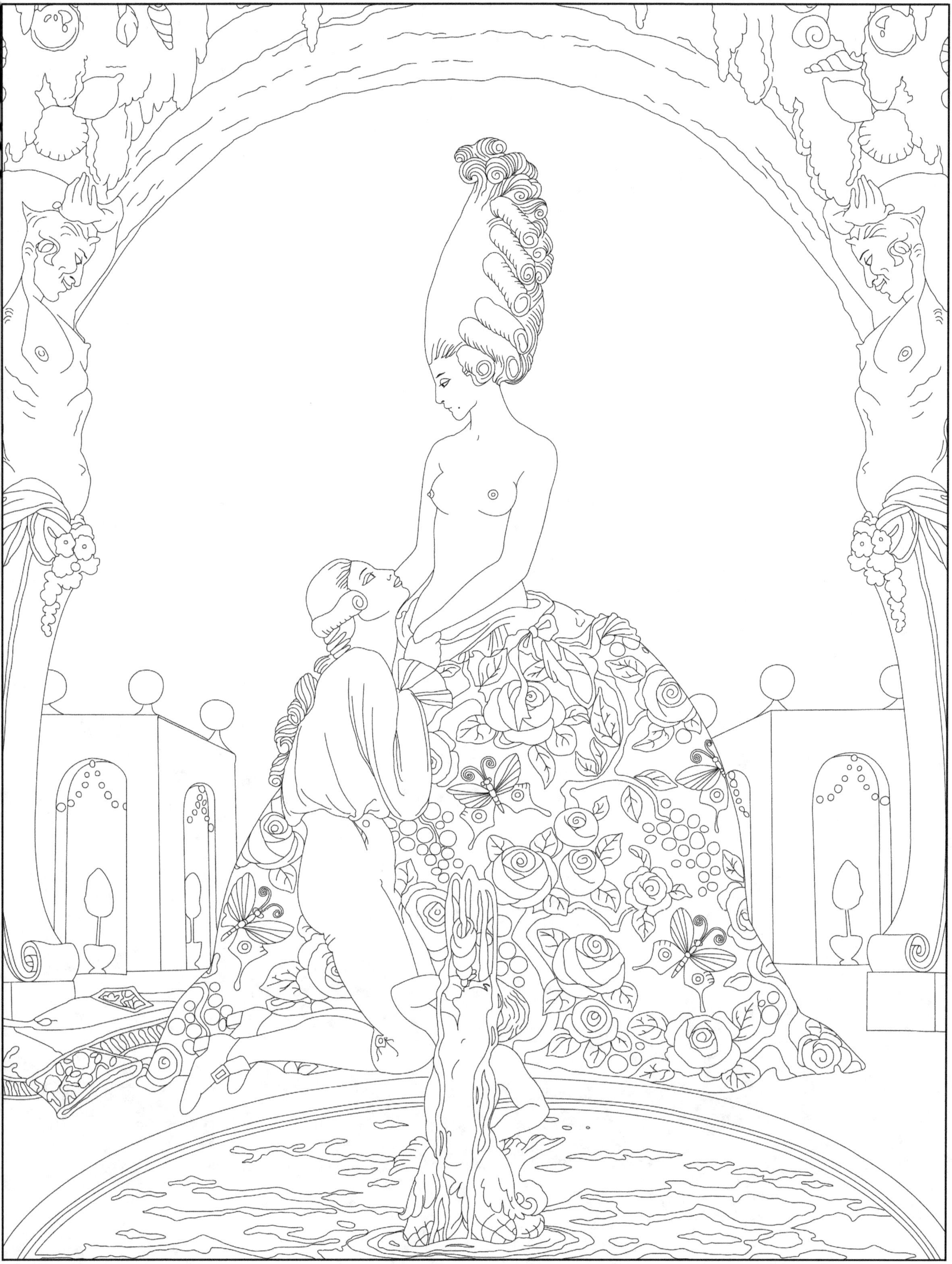

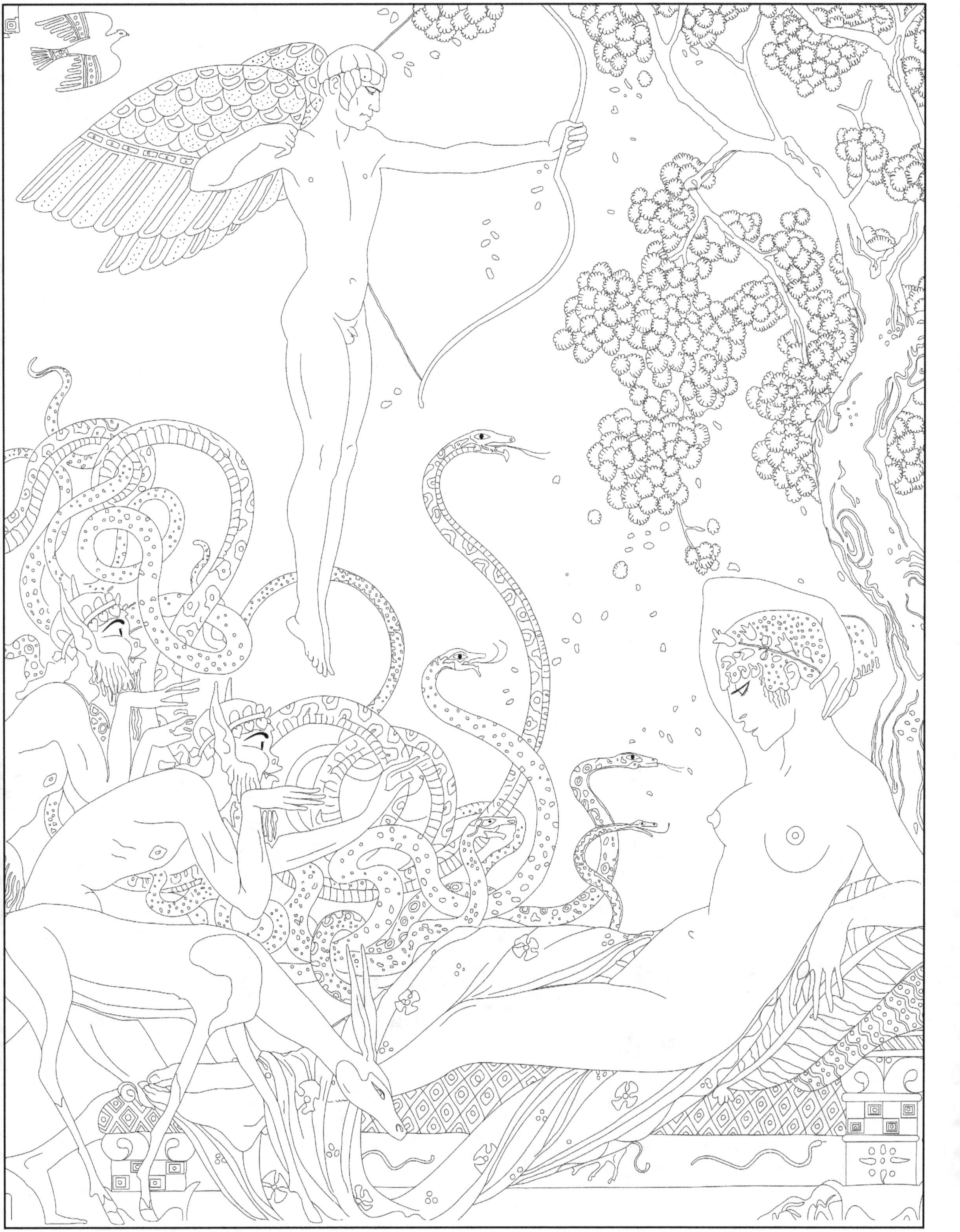

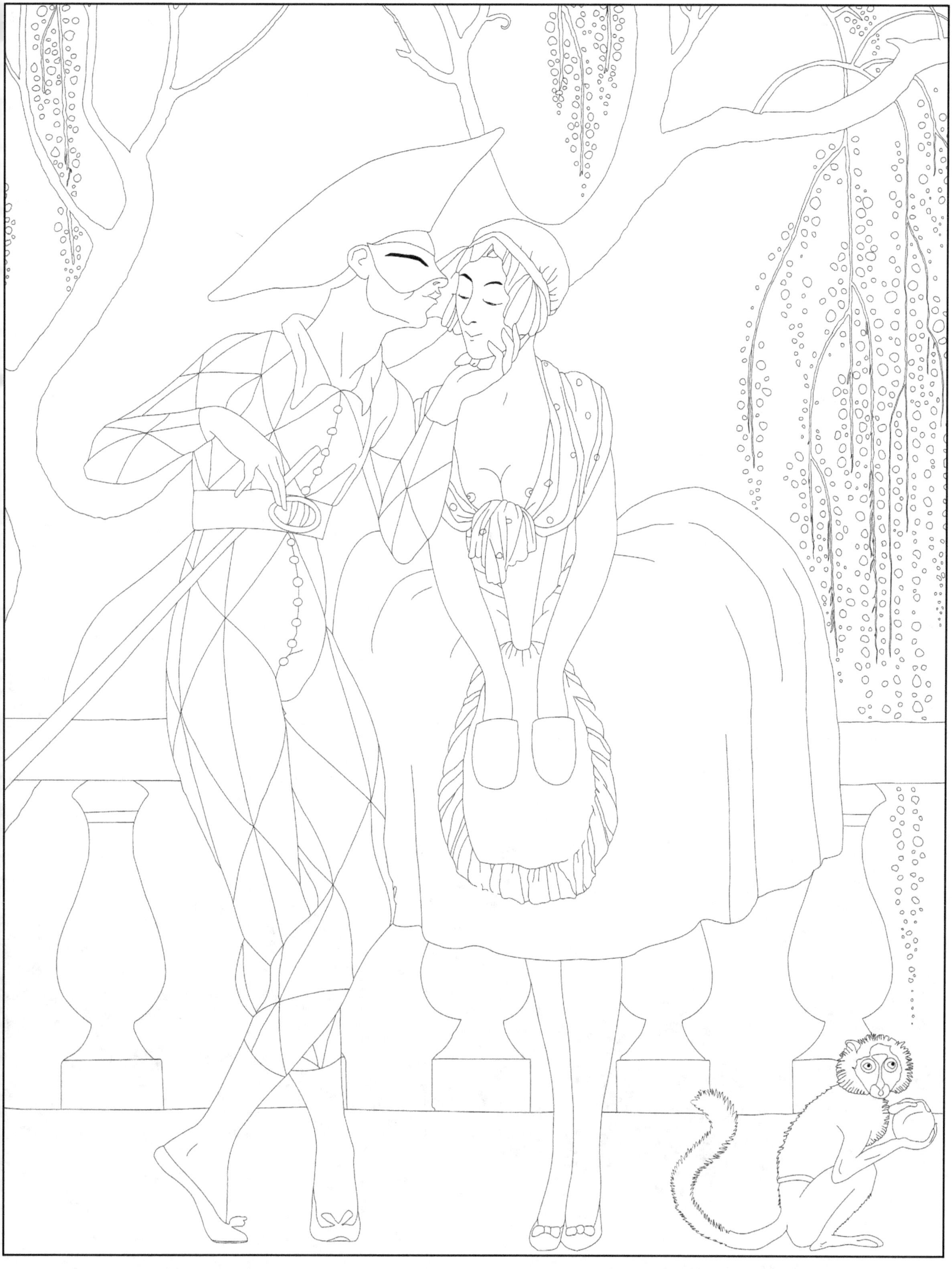

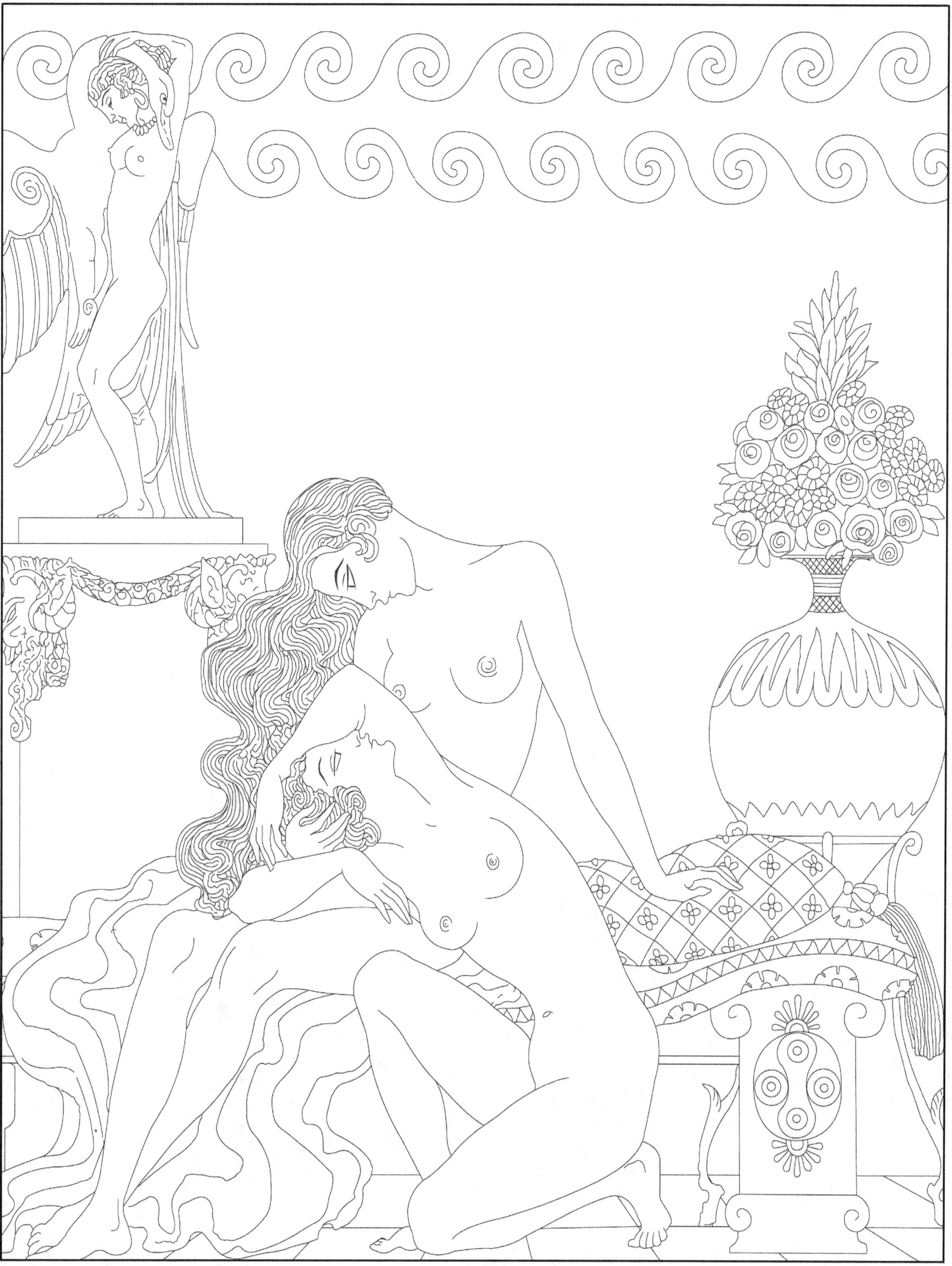

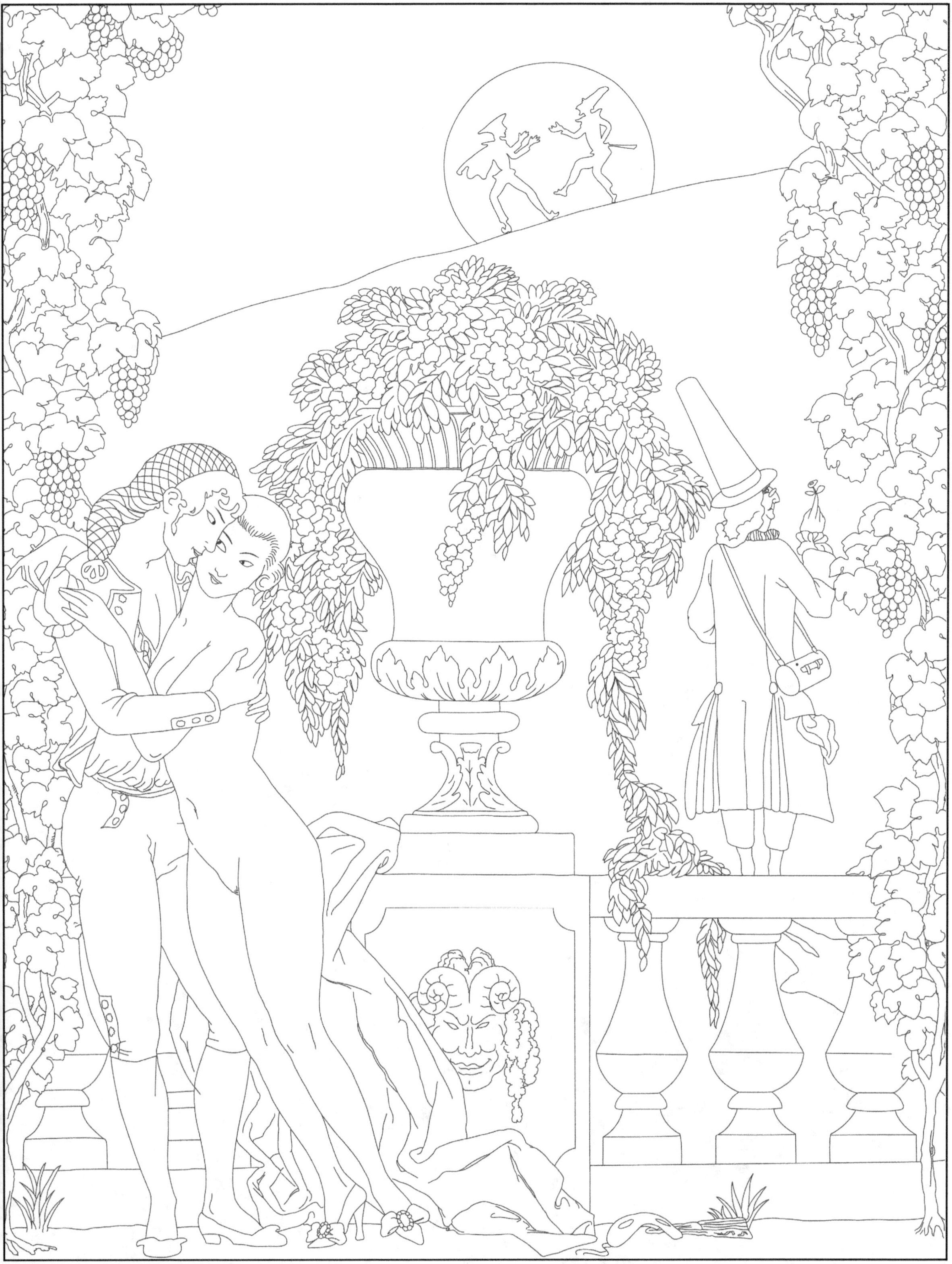

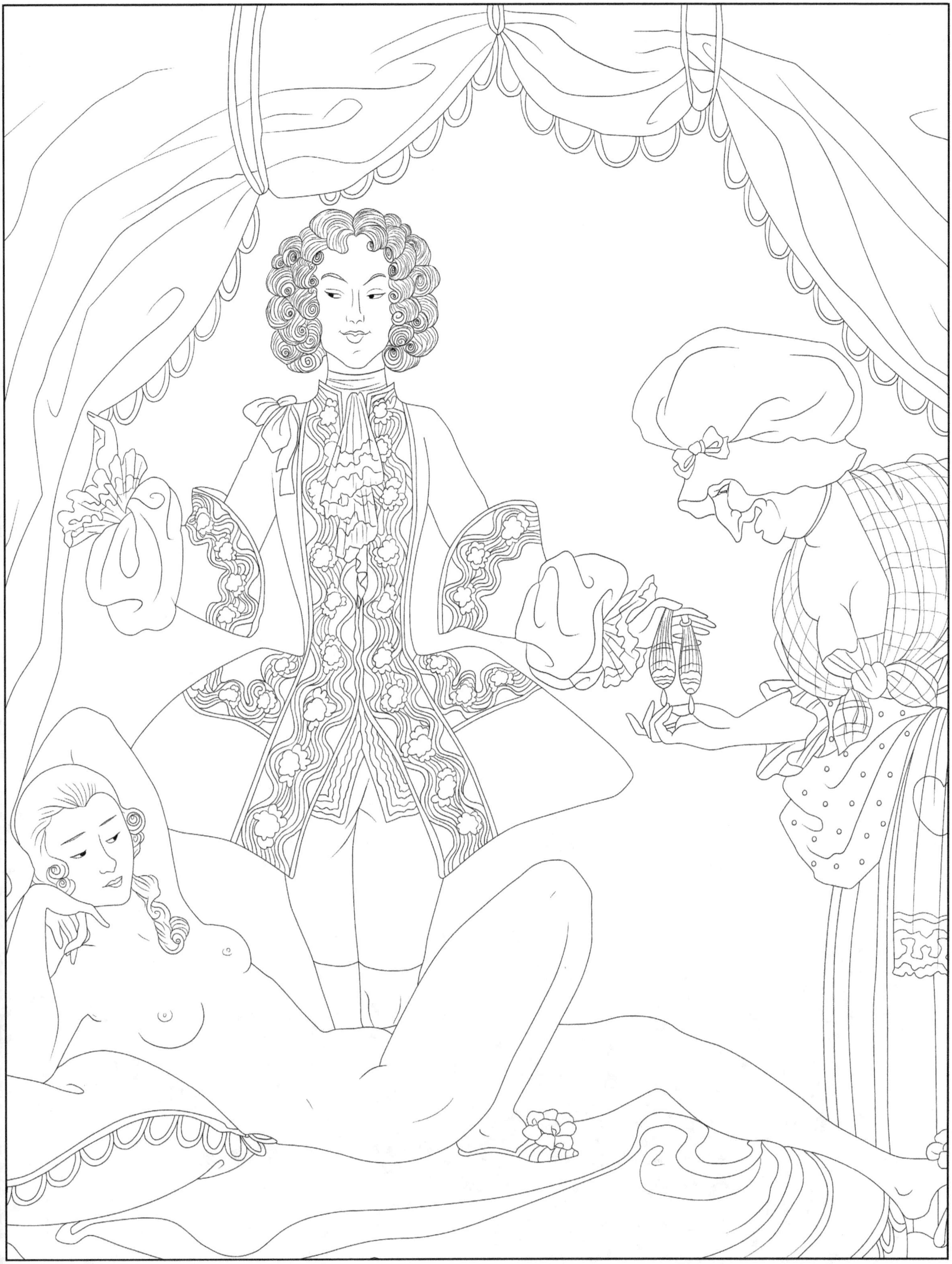

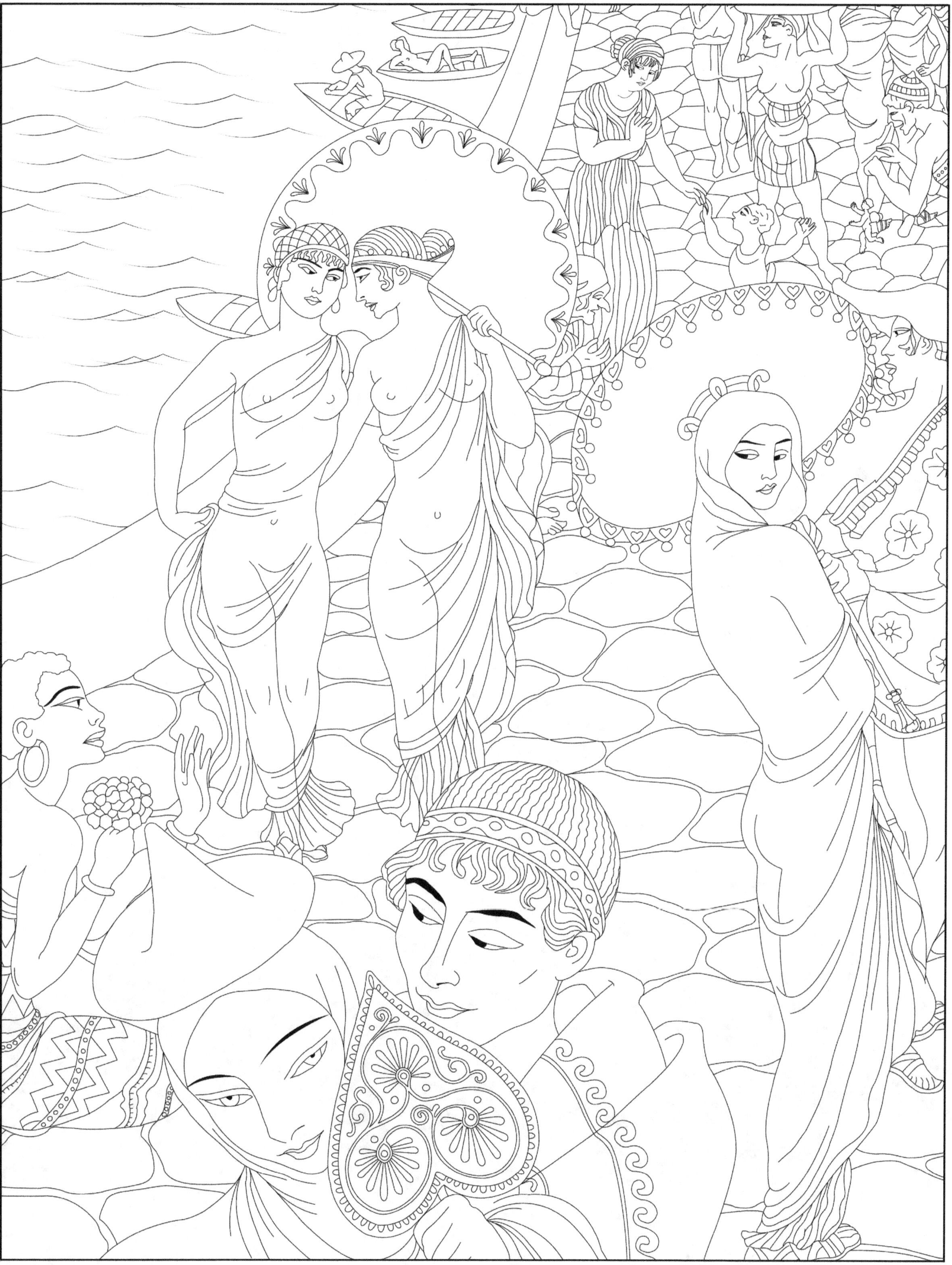

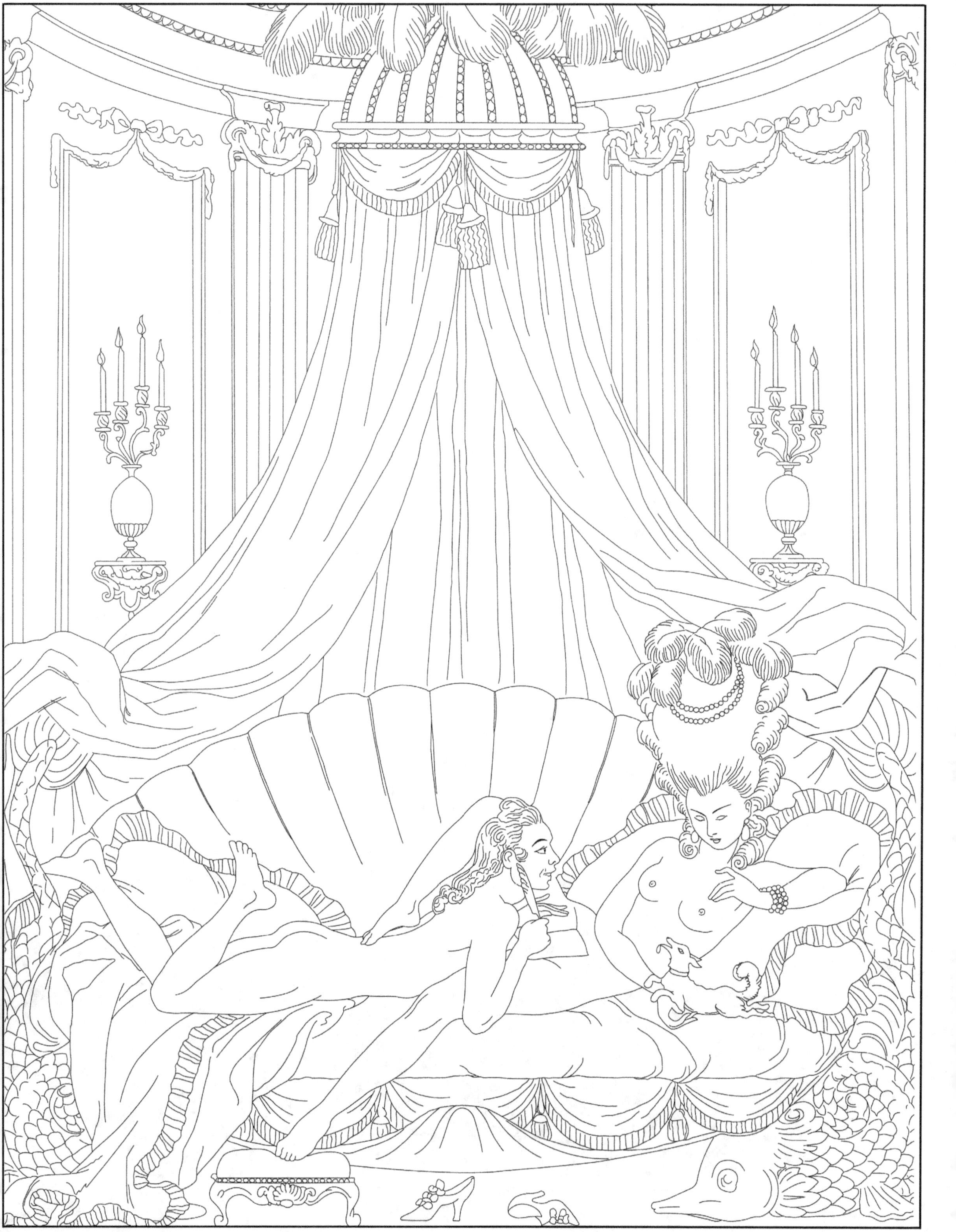

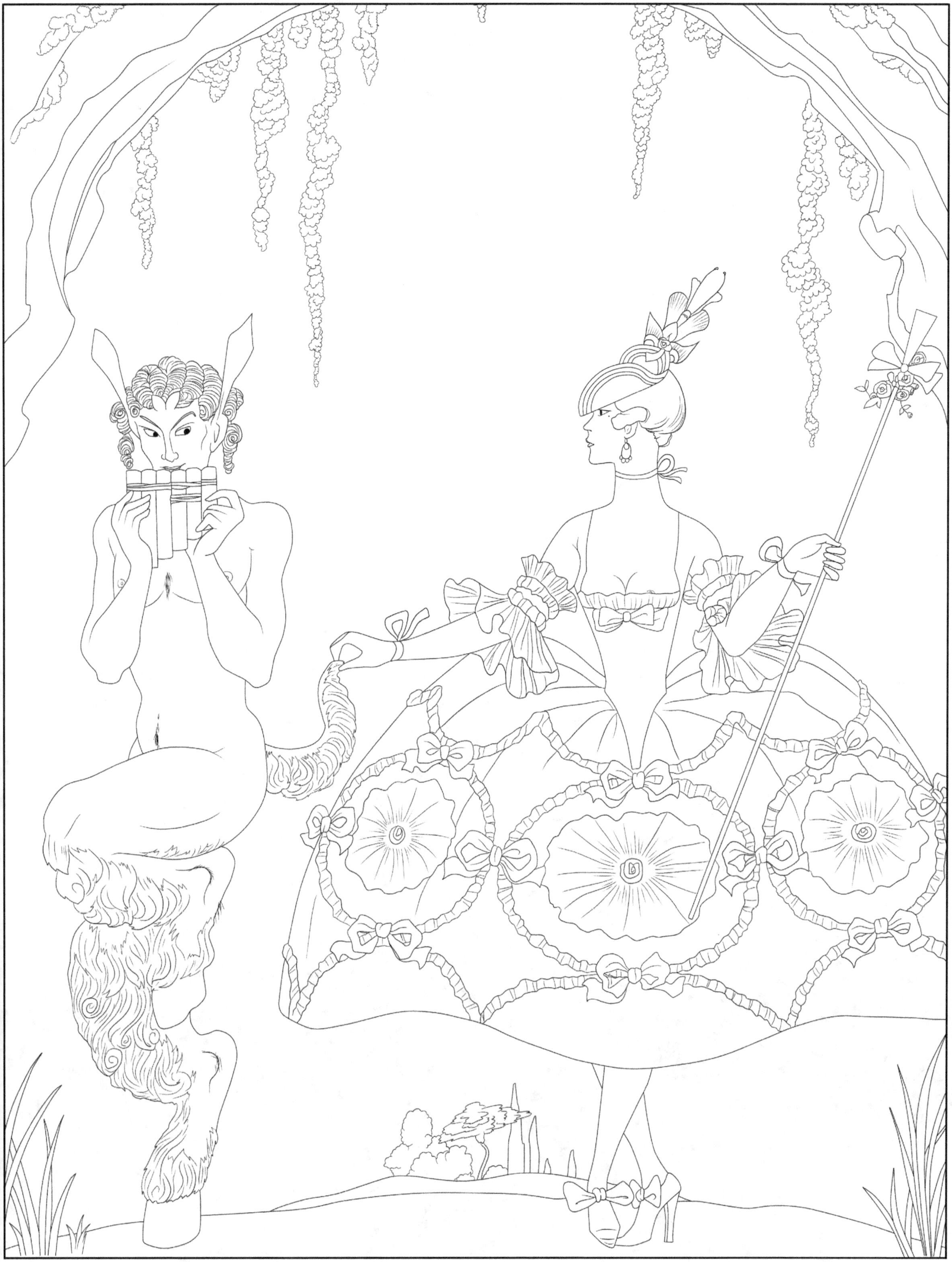

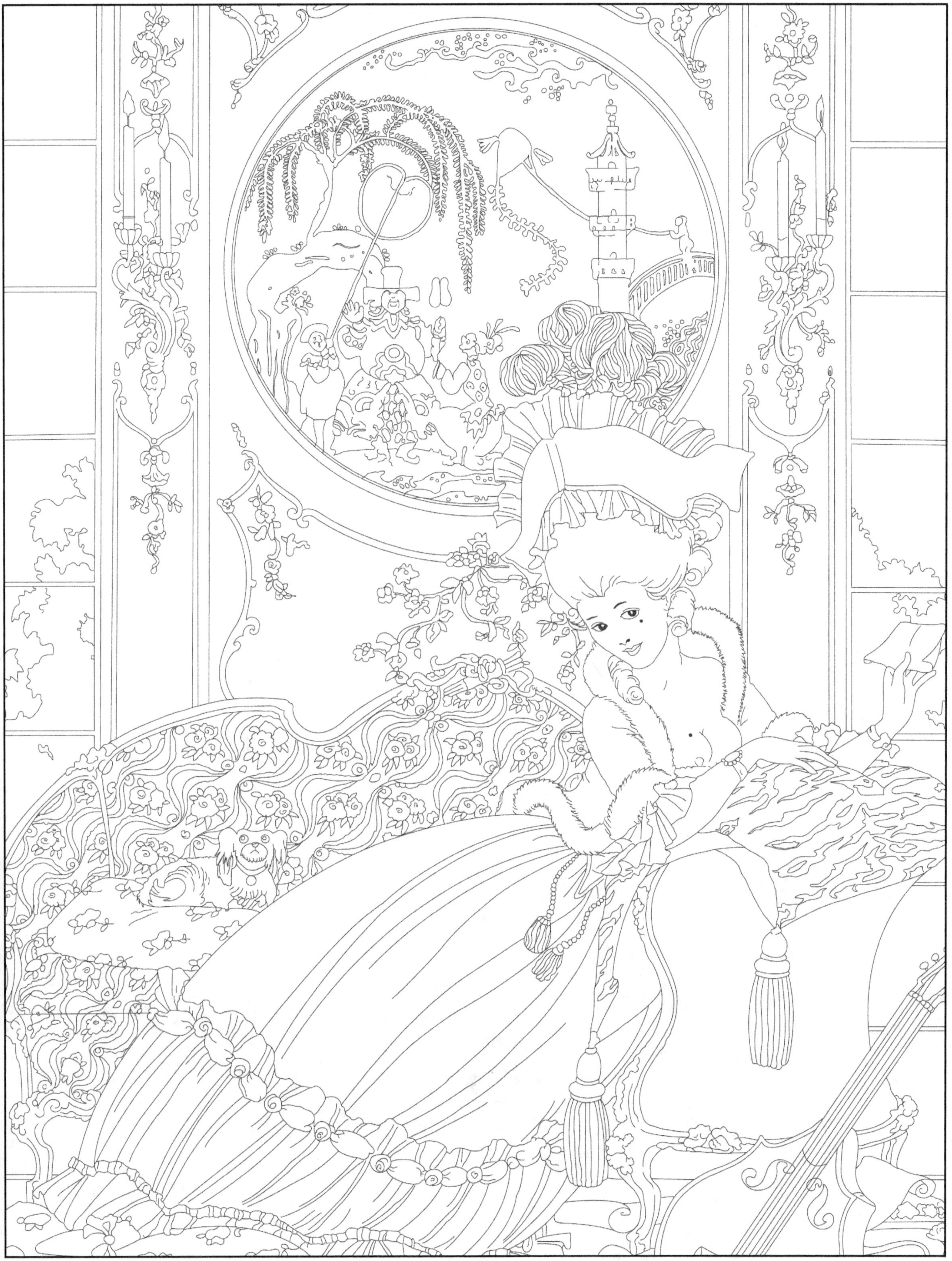

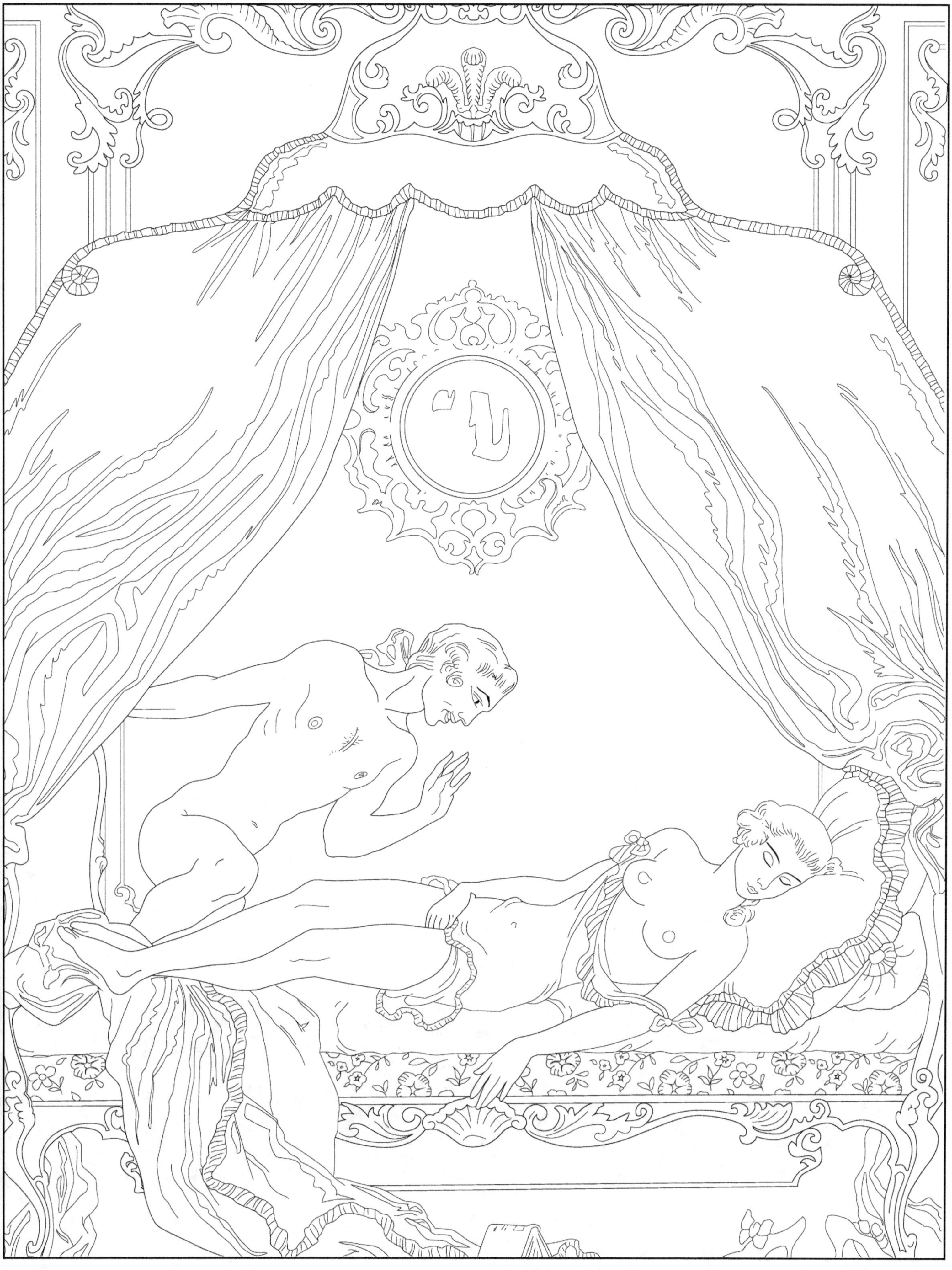

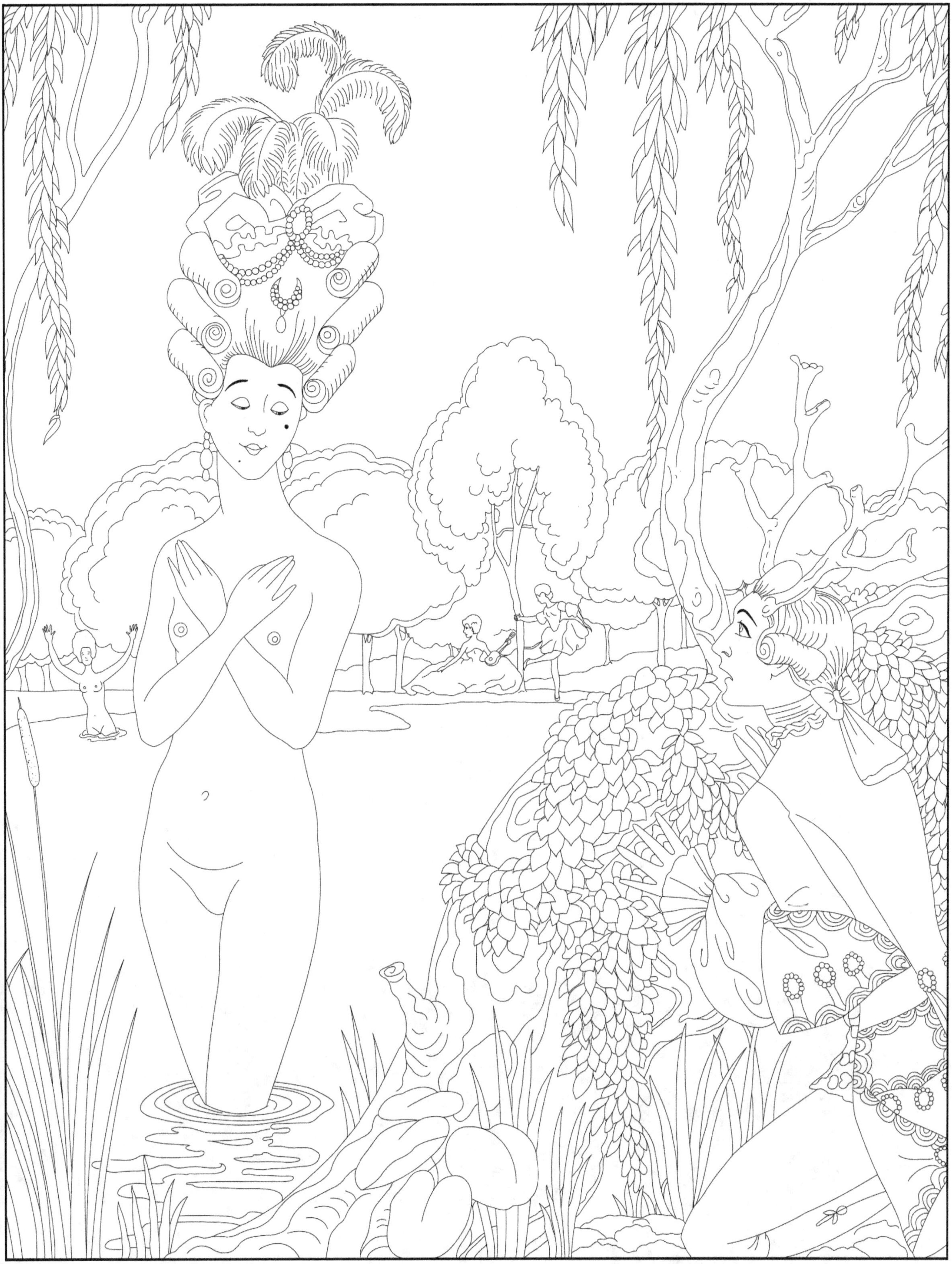

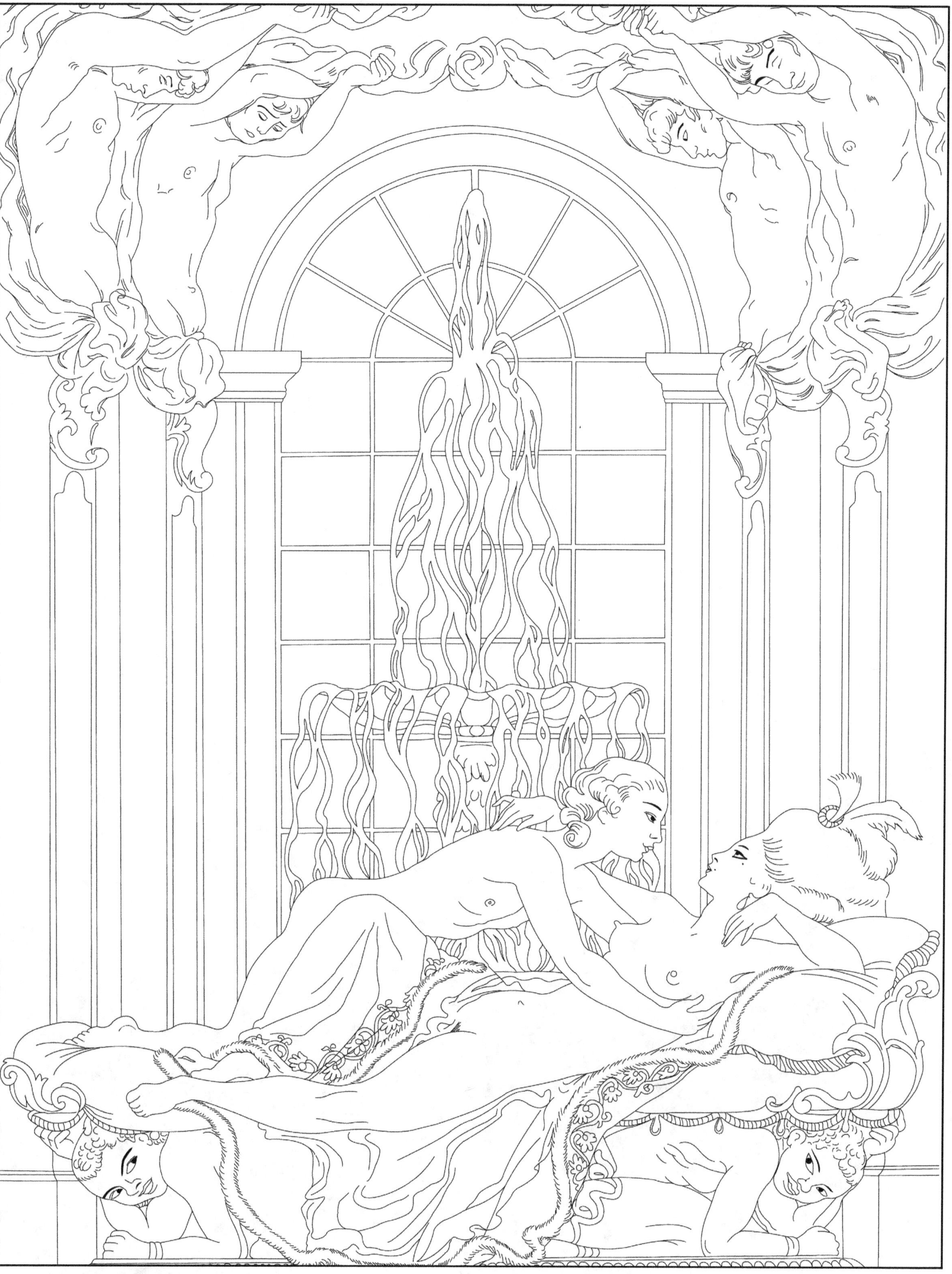

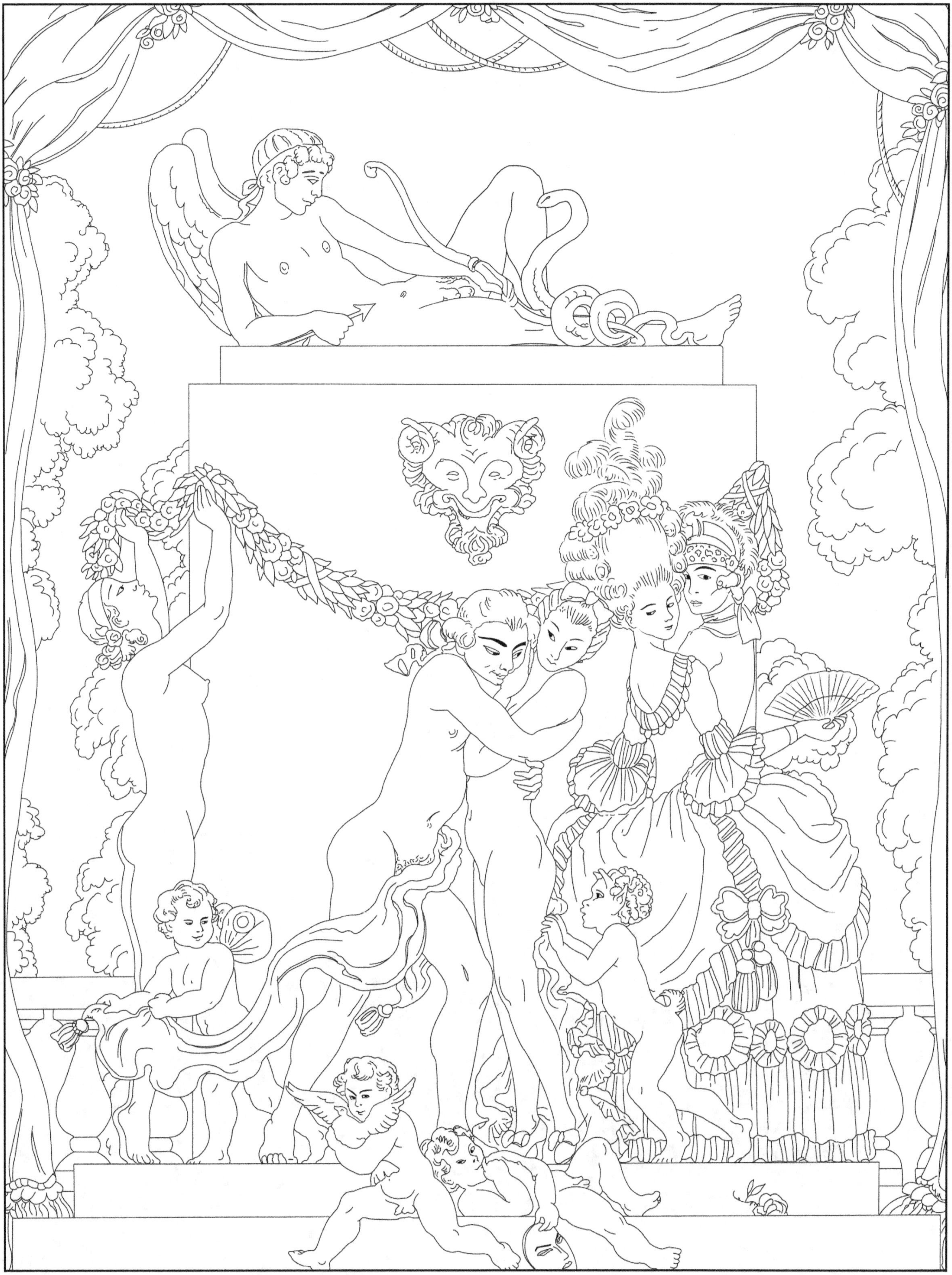

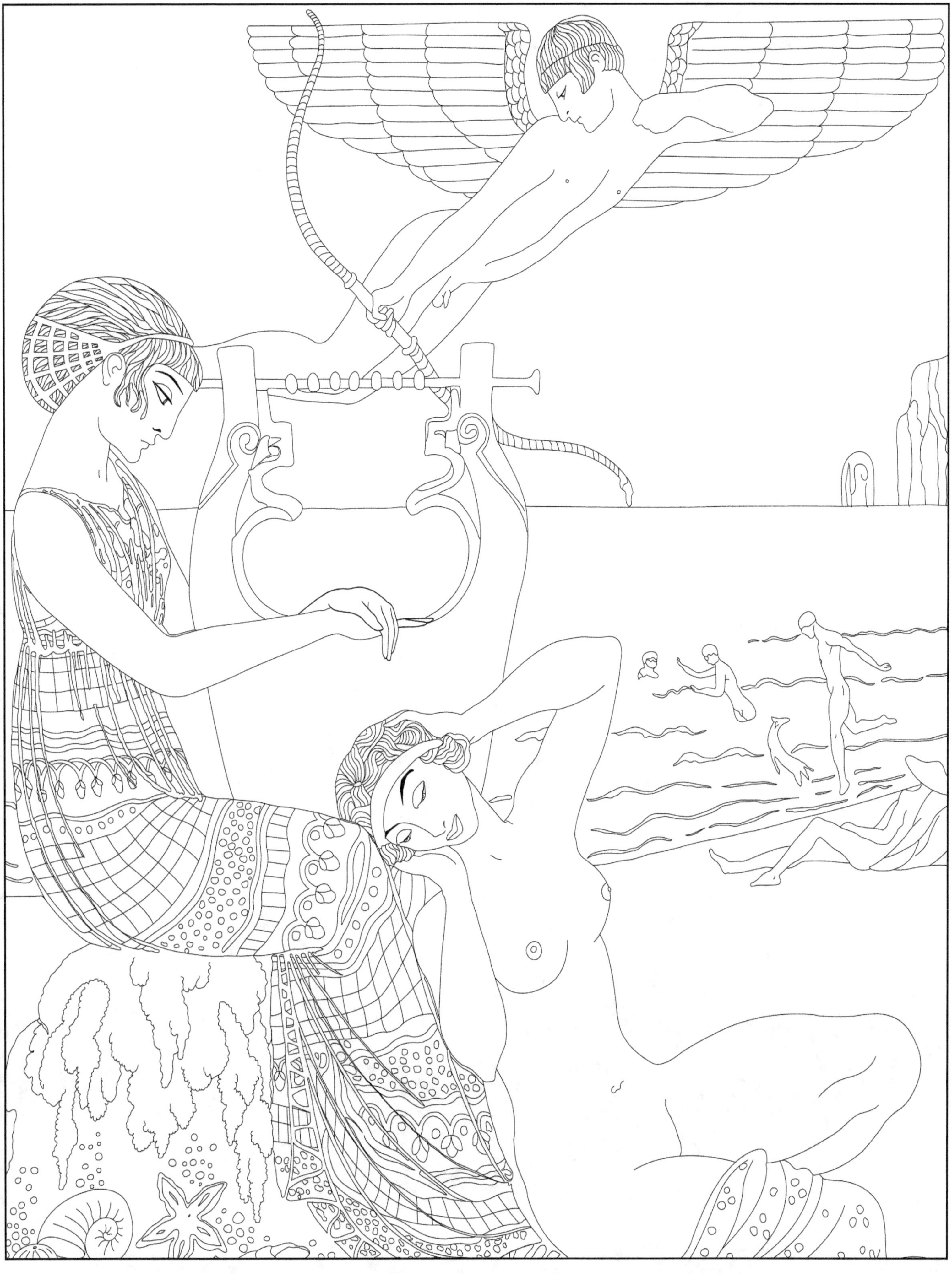

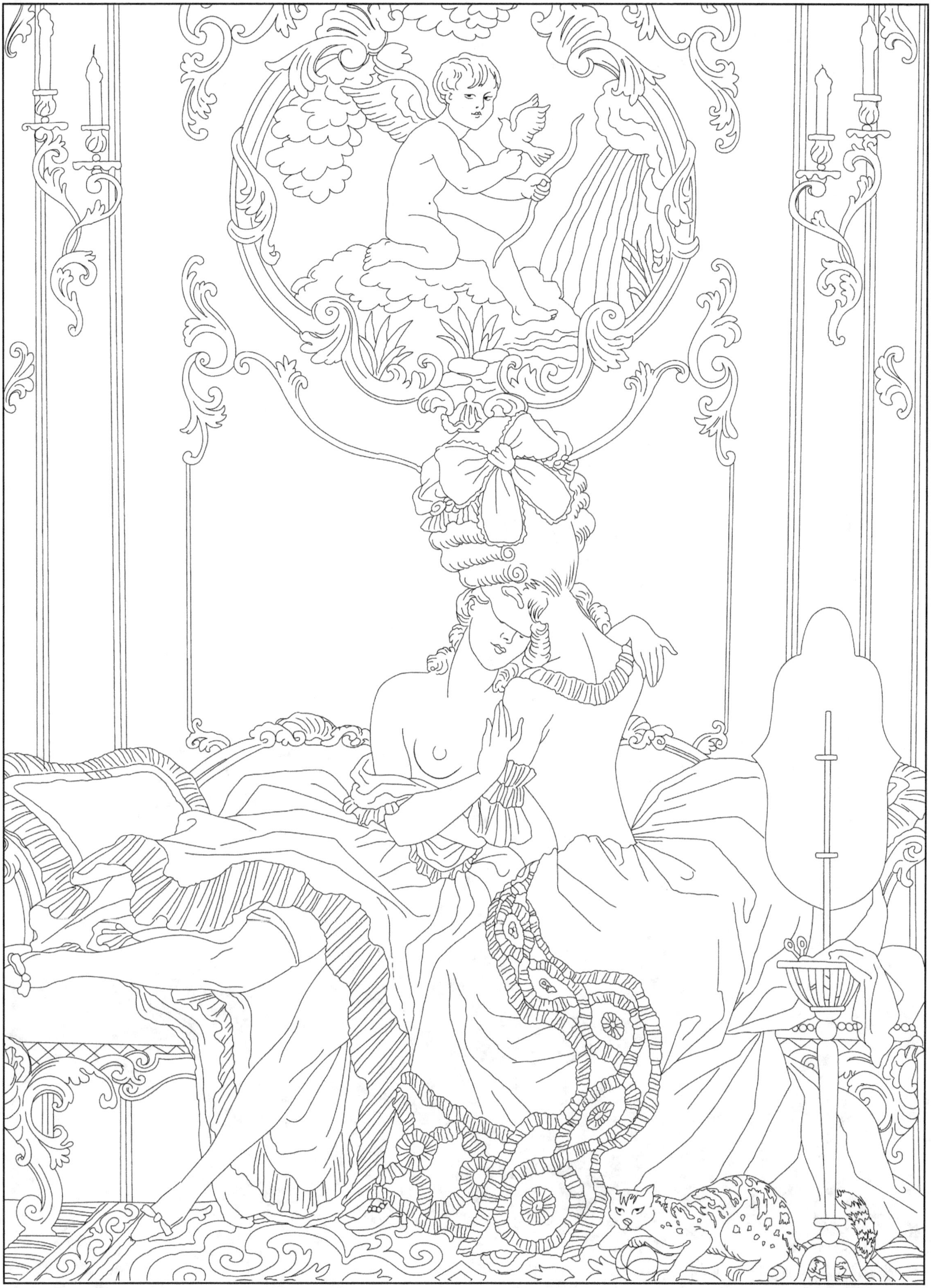

www.ingramcontent.com/pod-product-compliance
Lightning Source LLC
Chambersburg PA
CBHW081621220526
45468CB00010B/2980
* 9 7 8 1 8 8 7 5 9 3 6 1 8 *